1/3/85

The Gospel Passions

The
Gospel
Passions

GEOFFREY CHAPMAN
LONDON

A Geoffrey Chapman book published by
Cassell Ltd
1 Vincent Square, London SW1P 2PN

Concordat cum originali: John P. Dewis
Nihil obstat: Anton Cowan
Imprimatur: Monsignor Ralph Brown, V.G.,
                           Westminster, 4 October 1984

First published 1985

ISBN 0 225 66406 2

The version of Scripture used is the *Jerusalem Bible*, copyrighted © in 1966, 1967 and 1968
by Darton, Longman and Todd Ltd. and Doubleday and Company Inc., and used by permission.

Approved by the Australian Episcopal Liturgical Commission:
Concordat cum originali: Denis J. Hart
Imprimatur: + Edward B. Clancy DD LSS
                            Archbishop of Sydney, 15 October 1984

For use in the dioceses of the United States of America:
The Passion narratives, arranged for dramatic proclamation, are taken from the *Jerusalem Bible*
translation approved for use in the liturgy by the National Conference of Catholic Bishops (United States
of America) in plenary assembly in November 1968 and confirmed by decree of the Sacred Congregation
of Rites, December 9, 1968 (Prot. N. 2709/68). Published by authority of the Bishops' Committee on the
Liturgy, National Conference of Catholic Bishops (United States of America).

Typographical design by James Butler MSIAD
Typeset by Wyvern Typesetting Ltd, Bristol
Printed in Great Britain at The Beacon Press, Lewes and bound by
Hunter & Foulis Ltd, Edinburgh

Contents

Introduction

There are three ways in which one can read the Gospel accounts of the Lord's Passion: as a meditation, as a proclamation, and as a drama. The Church in its liturgy uses all three methods, and has done so for many centuries.

The earliest eye-witness account we have of the liturgy of Holy Week centres on Jerusalem, the place where Jesus died. It is written by a pilgrim to that city around the year 400 A.D. Her name was Egeria (variously spelt) and she describes how the citizens of Jerusalem commemorated the events of Holy Week. From noon until 3 p.m. on Good Friday they assembled on the Mount of the Crucifixion and listened to a succession of readings from the scriptures, culminating in the reading of 'the last moments of Jesus' from St John's Gospel. This was clearly a service of meditation.

The peoples of Northern Europe, with their genius for drama as evidenced in their mystery, or miracle, plays, must have exploited the dramatic possibilities of the accounts of the Passion very early on. We know that in the tenth century the liturgical rendering of the Passion by three singers and chorus was well established, and in medieval Europe we have evidence of the performance of extra-liturgical Passion Plays.

Rome preferred the method of proclamation by the deacon, and retained this tradition until well into the fourteenth century (*Ordo Romanus XV*, 60).

It is impossible to read the four Gospel accounts of the Passion without being struck by their dramatic quality, and we would expect this, for they are recounting the greatest drama that ever took place on the stage of human history. The habit of modern script-writers (as no doubt of the earlier compilers of Passion Plays) is to take elements from all four Gospels and string them together to form a more or less chronological sequence of events. The liturgy does not do that. It remains faithful to the written Gospel. Though all four evangelists are recounting the same event, each has his own style, his own viewpoint, his own purpose in writing, and his own policy in selecting and arranging the historical material as best to serve his ultimate purpose. That is to say, each Passion narrative has its own particular character which is respected by the liturgy.

St Matthew, writing no doubt for a Jewish audience, presents Jesus as the longed-for Messiah. His whole Gospel is a *proclamation* of that Jesus who came not to abolish the Law and the Prophets but to fulfil them. He is at pains to show that all the events of the passion are a fulfilment of the scriptures. Jesus was the 'suffering servant' of Yahweh as portrayed by the Prophet Isaiah. He was silent in the presence of his foes. His betrayal for thirty pieces of silver fulfilled the prophecy of Jeremiah. His whole passion is set in the context of Psalm 21 (22) – 'My God, my God, why have you deserted me' – the psalm of victory through suffering and death.

St Mark's Passion is concise and factual. Of all the passion narratives it is the most *dramatic*, bringing out the sharp antagonisms between the characters, their noisy and conflicting emotions, and, at the centre of the storm, the almost silent figure of Jesus, whose words, because they are so few and so highly charged, greatly increase the dramatic tension. This tension is finally released in the centurion's profession of faith: 'In truth this man was a son of God.'

St Luke's account is predominantly *meditative*. He is captivated by the character of Jesus and presents him in his most divinely human qualities: needing an angel from heaven to console him and yet superbly dignified, showing mercy to everyone, including his enemies, working a miracle to heal the soldier's ear, turning to look with compassion on the apostle who disowned him, promising paradise to the repentant thief, and in calmness and peace committing his soul to God. 'This was a great and good man.'

It is not so easy to classify St John's Passion. It lends itself to meditative reading and yet at the same time it is highly dramatic and proclaims unequivocally the divinity of Jesus. It consists of a series of dramatic dialogues: Jesus and his captors, Jesus and Annas, Jesus and Pilate, Pilate and the Chief Priests. Every dialogue is a vindication of the power and divinity of Jesus. His captors fall to the ground. Annas is confounded and reduced to silence. Pilate, the sceptic, is convinced of his innocence and seeks to free him. Even when he feels himself constrained by the threats of the Chief Priests to pronounce sentence of death on Jesus, he makes his point by proclaiming him King of the Jews. In every episode of his passion Jesus is master, even in death when, having bequeathed his mother to John and drunk the last cup of bitterness, he cries out 'It is accomplished' and gives up his spirit.

In addition, St John's Passion is the liturgical proclamation of the sacrifice of Christ. It is set in the context of the Jewish Passover Feast: Jesus is the Lamb of God, sacrificed for the sins of the world. As the lamb of sacrifice, not a bone of his body is broken. From his pierced side flow the healing streams of blood and water.

This present book is designed to enhance the liturgical proclamation of the Lord's passion, death and resurrection in Holy Week. Clearly, the options are many, ranging from a simple reading by the deacon or priest, to a highly dramatised version in full costume and involving, perhaps, 'chorus' groups of children and young people. It is not right to say that any one mode of presentation is more 'liturgical' than another. Much will depend on the mood, character and resources of the celebrating community. For example, a simple, meditative reading of St John's Passion on Good Friday has often proved highly effective and deeply moving.

Active participation does not necessarily mean that everybody in the church must have a part, but it does mean that everyone must feel personally involved. Hence in presenting the Passion, in whatever form, thought must be given to the best possible means of fostering this involvement. Good speakers are essential and they must have rehearsed their parts beforehand, otherwise they will produce between them a crop of distractions. Just as overacting and ham-acting is an annoyance in the presentation of plays, so it is possible to 'over-speak' and 'ham-speak' parts in a dramatic reading. The reader must feel his or her way into the role and produce as nearly as possible the nuance of meaning and emotion that is intended by the author.

A frequent source of distraction is a bad public-address system or its misuse. One often finds that only one microphone is provided for three speakers, with the result that the reading comes across at different levels of audibility. A discreet musical background to some parts of the reading may be highly effective, provided the music does not distract from the words, but rather enhances them. Music should not 'overload' the proclamation in any way.

Slides, too, can add a further dimension and help to rivet attention if they are projected at a suitable place in the church where they can be seen easily. They are most effective if they evoke the mood, rather than the action, of the narrative. It is very distracting to be shown the paintings of twenty different artists portraying twenty different Christs in as many different locations.

Sometimes in the past we may have been tempted to regard the long reading of the Passion in Holy Week as a penance to be endured. That is not the intention of the liturgy. It is an invitation to become more whole-heartedly united with Christ in his redeeming passion.

Harold Winstone

Note

The name of each speaker is given in the margin throughout; often, however, all the parts other than Narrator, Jesus and Crowd will be taken by one reader only.
The symbols ▶ and ◀ indicate the beginning and end of the shorter form of the reading where appropriate.

Passion Sunday [Palm Sunday]

YEAR A

The passion of our Lord Jesus Christ
according to Matthew   26:14 – 27:66

Narrator	One of the Twelve, the man called Judas Iscariot, went to the chief priests and said:
Judas	What are you prepared to give me if I hand him over to you?
Narrator	They paid him thirty silver pieces, and from that moment he looked for an opportunity to betray him.
	Now on the first day of Unleavened Bread the disciples came to Jesus to say,
Crowd	Where do you want us to make the preparations for you to eat the passover?
Narrator	He replied:
Jesus	**Go to so-and-so in the city and say to him, 'The Master says: My time is near. It is at your house that I am keeping Passover with my disciples'.**
Narrator	The disciples did what Jesus told them and prepared the Passover. When the evening came he was at table with the twelve disciples. And while they were eating he said:
Jesus	**I tell you solemnly, one of you is about to betray me.**
Narrator	They were greatly distressed and started asking him in turn,
Crowd	Not I, Lord, surely?
Narrator	He answered:
Jesus	**Someone who has dipped his hand into the dish with me, will betray me. The Son of Man is going to his fate, as the scriptures say he will, but alas for that man by whom the Son of Man is betrayed! Better for that man if he had never been born!**
Narrator	Judas, who was to betray him, asked in his turn,
Judas	Not I, Rabbi, surely?
Narrator	Jesus answered:
Jesus	**They are your own words.**
Narrator	Now as they were eating, Jesus took some bread, and when he had said the blessing he broke it and gave it to the disciples and said:
Jesus	**Take it and eat; this is my body.**
Narrator	Then he took a cup, and when he had returned thanks he gave it to them saying:
Jesus	**Drink all of you from this, for this is my blood, the blood of the covenant, which is to be poured out for many for the forgiveness of sins. From now on, I tell you, I shall not drink wine until the day I drink the new wine with you in the kingdom of my Father.**

I

Narrator	After psalms had been sung they left for the Mount of Olives. Then Jesus said to them,
Jesus	**You will all lose faith in me this night, for the scripture says: I shall strike the shepherd and the sheep of the flock will be scattered. But after my resurrection I shall go before you to Galilee.**
Narrator	At this, Peter said:
Peter	Though all lose faith in you, I will never lose faith.
Narrator	Jesus answered him,
Jesus	**I tell you solemnly, this very night, before the cock crows, you will have disowned me three times.**
Narrator	Peter said to him,
Peter	Even if I have to die with you, I will never disown you.
Narrator	And all the disciples said the same.
	Then Jesus came with them to a small estate called Gethsemane; and he said to his disciples,
Jesus	**Stay here while I go over there to pray.**
Narrator	He took Peter and the two sons of Zebedee with him. And sadness came over him, and great distress. Then he said to them:
Jesus	**My soul is sorrowful to the point of death. Wait here and keep awake with me.**
Narrator	And going on a little further he fell on his face and prayed:
Jesus	**My Father, if it is possible let this cup pass me by. Nevertheless, let it be as you, not I, would have it.**
Narrator	He came back to the disciples and found them sleeping, and he said to Peter:
Jesus	**So you had not the strength to keep awake with me one hour? You should be awake, and praying not to be put to the test. The spirit is willing, but the flesh is weak.**
Narrator	Again, a second time, he went away and prayed:
Jesus	**My father, if this cup cannot pass by without my drinking it, your will be done!**
Narrator	And he came again back and found them sleeping, their eyes were so heavy. Leaving them there, he went away again and prayed for the third time, repeating the same words. Then he came back to the disciples and said to them,
Jesus	**You can sleep on now and take your rest. Now the hour has come when the Son of Man is to be betrayed into the hands of sinners. Get up! Let us go! My betrayer is already close at hand.**
Narrator	He was still speaking when Judas, one of the Twelve, appeared, and with him a large number of men armed with swords and clubs, sent by the chief priests and elders of the people. Now the traitor had arranged a sign with them. He had said:
Judas	'The one I kiss, he is the man. Take him in charge.'
Narrator	So he went straight up to Jesus and said:
Judas	Greetings, Rabbi,
Narrator	and kissed him. Jesus said to him,

2

Jesus	**My friend, do what you are here for.**
Narrator	Then they came forward, seized Jesus and took him in charge. At that, one of the followers of Jesus grasped his sword and drew it; he struck out at the high priest's servant, and cut off his ear. Jesus then said:
Jesus	**Put your sword back, for all who draw the sword will die by the sword. Or do you think that I cannot appeal to my Father who would promptly send more than twelve legions of angels to my defence? But then, how would the scriptures be fulfilled that say this is the way it must be?**
Narrator	It was at this time that Jesus said to the crowds:
Jesus	**Am I a brigand, that you had to set out to capture me with swords and clubs? I sat teaching in the Temple day after day and you never laid hands on me.**
Narrator	Now all this happened to fulfil the prophecies in scripture. Then all the disciples deserted him and ran away.
	The men who had arrested Jesus led him off to Caiaphas the high priest, where the scribes and the elders were assembled. Peter followed him at a distance, and when he reached the high priest's palace, he went in and sat down with the attendants to see what the end would be.
	The chief priests and the whole Sanhedrin were looking for evidence against Jesus, however false, on which they might pass the death-sentence. But they could not find any, though several lying witnesses came forward. Eventually two stepped forward and made a statement,
Crowd	This man said: 'I have power to destroy the Temple of God and in three days build it up'.
Narrator	The high priest then stood up and said to him:
High priest	Have you no answer to that? What is this evidence these men are bringing against you?
Narrator	But Jesus was silent. And the high priest said to him:
High priest	I put you on oath by the living God to tell us if you are the Christ, the Son of God.
Narrator	Jesus answered:
Jesus	**The words are your own. Moreover, I tell you that from this time onward you will see the Son of Man seated at the right hand of the Power and coming on the clouds of heaven.**
Narrator	At this, the high priest tore his clothes and said:
High priest	He has blasphemed. What need of witnesses have we now? There! You have just heard the blasphemy. What is your opinion?
Narrator	They answered:
Crowd	He deserves to die.
Narrator	Then they spat in his face and hit him with their fists; others said as they struck him:
Crowd	Play the prophet, Christ! Who hit you then?
Narrator	Meanwhile Peter was sitting outside in the courtyard, and a servant-girl came up to him and said:

3

Servant-girl 1	You too were with Jesus the Galilean.
Narrator	But he denied it in front of them all, saying:
Peter	I do not know what you are talking about.
Narrator	When he went out to the gateway another servant-girl saw him and said to the people there:
Servant-girl 2	This man was with Jesus the Nazarene.
Narrator	And again, with an oath, he denied it,
Peter	I do not know the man.
Narrator	A little later the bystanders came up and said to Peter:
Crowd	You are one of them for sure! Why, your accent gives you away.
Narrator	Then he started calling down curses on himself and swearing:
Peter	I do not know the man.
Narrator	At that moment the cock crew, and Peter remembered what Jesus had said, 'Before the cock crows you will have disowned me three times.' And he went outside and wept bitterly.

When morning came, all the chief priests and the elders of the people met in council to bring about the death of Jesus. They had him bound, and led him away to hand him over to Pilate, the governor. When he found that Jesus had been condemned, Judas his betrayer was filled with remorse and took the thirty pieces of silver back to the chief priests and elders, saying:

Judas	I have sinned. I have betrayed innocent blood.
Narrator	They replied:
Crowd	What is that to us? That is your concern.
Narrator	And flinging down the silver pieces in the sanctuary he made off, and went and hanged himself. The chief priests picked up the silver pieces and said:
Crowd	It is against the Law to put this into the treasury; it is blood money.
Narrator	So they discussed the matter and bought the potter's field with it as a graveyard for foreigners, and this is why the field is called the Field of Blood today. The words of the prophet Jeremiah were then fulfilled: And they took the thirty silver pieces, the sum at which the precious One was priced by children of Israel, and they gave them for the potter's field, just as the Lord directed me.

▶Jesus, then, was brought before the governor, and the governor put to him this question:

Pilate	Are you the king of the Jews?
Narrator	Jesus replied:
Jesus	**It is you who say it.**
Narrator	But when he was accused by the chief priests and the elders he refused to answer at all. Pilate then said to him:
Pilate	Do you not hear how many charges they have brought against you?
Narrator	But to the governor's complete amazement, he offered no reply to any of the charges.

At festival time it was the governor's practice to release a prisoner for the people, anyone they chose. Now there was at that time a notorious prisoner whose name was Barabbas. So when the crowd gathered, Pilate said to them,

Pilate	Which do you want me to release for you: Barabbas or Jesus who is called Christ?
Narrator	For Pilate knew it was out of jealousy that they had handed him over. Now as he was seated in the chair of judgement, his wife sent him a message,
Pilate's wife	Have nothing to do with that man; I have been upset all day by a dream I had about him.
Narrator	The chief priests and the elders, however, had persuaded the crowd to demand the release of Barabbas and the execution of Jesus. So when the governor spoke and asked them:
Pilate	Which of the two do you want me to release for you?
Narrator	They said:
Crowd	Barabbas.
Narrator	Pilate said to them:
Pilate	What am I to do with Jesus who is called Christ?
Narrator	They all said:
Crowd	Let him be crucified!
Narrator	Pilate asked:
Pilate	Why? What harm has he done?
Narrator	But they shouted all the louder,
Crowd	Let him be crucified!
Narrator	Then Pilate saw that he was making no impression, that in fact a riot was imminent. So he took some water, washed his hands in front of the crowd and said:
Pilate	I am innocent of this man's blood. It is your concern.
Narrator	And the people, to a man, shouted back:
Crowd	His blood be on us and on our children!
Narrator	Then he released Barabbas for them. He ordered Jesus to be first scourged and then handed over to be crucified.
	The governor's soldiers took Jesus with them into the Praetorium and collected the whole cohort round him. Then they stripped him and made him wear a scarlet cloak, and having twisted some thorns into a crown they put this on his head and placed a reed in his right hand. To make fun of him they knelt to him saying:
Crowd	Hail, king of the Jews!
Narrator	And they spat on him and took the reed and struck him on the head with it. And when they had finished making fun of him, they took off the cloak and dressed him in his own clothes and led him away to crucify him.
	On their way out, they came across a man from Cyrene, Simon by name, and enlisted him to carry his cross. When they had reached a place called Golgotha, that is, the place of the skull, they gave him wine to drink. When they had finished crucifying him they shared out his clothing by casting lots, and then sat down and stayed there keeping guard over him. Above his head was placed the charge against him; it read: 'This is Jesus, the King of the Jews'. At the same time two robbers were crucified with him, one on the right and one on the left.

The passers-by jeered at him; they shook their heads and said:

Crowd   So you would destroy the Temple and rebuild it in three days! Then save yourself! If you are God's son, come down from the cross!

Narrator   The chief priests with the scribes and elders mocked him in the same way, saying:

Crowd   He saved others; he cannot save himself. He is the King of Israel; let him come down from the cross now, and we will believe in him. He put his trust in God; now let God rescue him if he wants him. For he did say, 'I am the son of God'.

Narrator   Even the robbers who were crucified with him taunted him in the same way.

From the sixth hour there was darkness over all the land until the ninth hour. And about the ninth hour, Jesus cried out in a loud voice:

Jesus   **Eli, Eli, lama sabachthani?**

Narrator   That is: 'My God, my God, why have you deserted me?' When some of those who stood there heard this, they said:

Crowd   The man is calling on Elijah,

Narrator   and one of them quickly ran to get a sponge which he dipped in vinegar and, putting it on a reed, gave it him to drink. The rest of them said:

Crowd   Wait! See if Elijah will come to save him.

Narrator   But Jesus, again crying out in a loud voice, yielded up his spirit.

All kneel and pause a moment.

Narrator   At that, the veil of the Temple was torn in two from top to bottom; the earth quaked; the rocks were split; the tombs opened and the bodies of many holy men rose from the dead, and these, after his resurrection, came out of the tombs, entered the Holy City and appeared to a number of people.

Meanwhile the centurion, together with the others guarding Jesus, had seen the earthquake and all that was taking place, and they were terrified and said:

Crowd   In truth this was a son of God. ◄

Narrator   And many women were there, watching from a distance, the same women who had followed Jesus from Galilee and looked after him. Among them were Mary of Magdala, Mary the mother of James and Joseph, and the mother of Zebedee's sons.

When it was evening, there came a rich man of Arimathaea called Joseph, who had himself become a disciple of Jesus. This man went to Pilate and asked for the body of Jesus. Pilate thereupon ordered it to be handed over. So Joseph took the body, wrapped it in a clean shroud and put it in his own new tomb which he had hewn out of the rock. He then rolled a large stone across the entrance of the tomb and went away. Now Mary of Magdala and the other Mary were there, sitting opposite the sepulchre.

Next day, that is, when Preparation Day was over, the chief priests and the Pharisees went in a body to Pilate and said to him,

Crowd   Your Excellency, we recall that this impostor said, while he was still alive, 'After three days I shall rise again'. Therefore give the order to have the sepulchre kept secure until the third day, for fear his disciples come and steal him away and tell the people, 'He has risen from the dead'. This last piece of fraud would be worse than what went before.

Narrator   Pilate said to them:

Pilate   You may have your guards. Go and make all as secure as you know how.

Narrator   So they went and made the sepulchre secure, putting seals on the stone and mounting a guard.

Passion Sunday [*Palm Sunday*]

YEAR B

*The passion of our Lord Jesus Christ
according to Mark*

14:1 – 15:47

Narrator	It was two days before the Passover and the feast of Unleavened Bread, and the chief priests and scribes were looking for a way to arrest Jesus by some trick and have him put to death. For they said,
Crowd	It must not be during the festivities, or there will be a disturbance among the people.
Narrator	Jesus was at Bethany in the house of Simon the leper; he was at dinner when a woman came in with an alabaster jar of very costly ointment, pure nard. She broke the jar and poured the ointment on his head. Some who were there said to one another indignantly,
Crowd	Why this waste of ointment? Ointment like this could have been sold for over three hundred denarii and the money given to the poor;
Narrator	and they were angry with her. But Jesus said,
Jesus	**Leave her alone. Why are you upsetting her? What she has done for me is one of the good works. You have the poor with you always and you can be kind to them whenever you wish, but you will not always have me. She has done what was in her power to do; she has anointed my body beforehand for its burial. I tell you solemnly, wherever throughout all the world the Good News is proclaimed, what she has done will be told also, in remembrance of her.**
Narrator	Judas Iscariot, one of the Twelve, approached the chief priests with an offer to hand Jesus over to them. They were delighted to hear it, and promised to give him money; and he looked for a way of betraying him when the opportunity should occur.
	On the first day of Unleavened Bread, when the Passover lamb was sacrificed, his disciples said to him,
Crowd	Where do you want us to go and make the preparations for you to eat the passover?
Narrator	So he sent two of his disciples, saying to them,
Jesus	**Go into the city and you will meet a man carrying a pitcher of water. Follow him, and say to the owner of the house which he enters, 'The Master says: Where is my dining room in which I can eat the passover with my disciples?' He will show you a large upper room furnished with couches, all prepared. Make the preparations for us there.**
Narrator	The disciples set out and went to the city and found everything as he had told them, and prepared the Passover.

8

	When evening came he arrived with the Twelve. And while they were at table eating, Jesus said,
Jesus	**I tell you solemnly, one of you is about to betray me, one of you eating with me.**
Narrator	They were distressed and asked him, one after another,
Crowd	Not I, surely?
Narrator	He said to them,
Jesus	**It is one of the Twelve, one who is dipping into the same dish with me. Yes, the Son of Man is going to his fate, as the scriptures say he will, but alas for that man by whom the Son of Man is betrayed! Better for that man if he had never been born!**
Narrator	And as they were eating he took some bread, and when he had said the blessing he broke it and gave it to them, saying,
Jesus	**Take it; this is my body.**
Narrator	Then he took a cup, and when he had returned thanks he gave it to them, and all drank from it, and he said to them,
Jesus	**This is my blood, the blood of the covenant, which is to be poured out for many. I tell you solemnly, I shall not drink any more wine until the day I drink the new wine in the kingdom of God.**
Narrator	After psalms had been sung they left for the Mount of Olives. And Jesus said to them,
Jesus	**You will all lose faith, for the scripture says, 'I shall strike the shepherd and the sheep will be scattered'. However after my resurrection I shall go before you to Galilee.**
Narrator	Peter said,
Peter	Even if all lose faith, I will not.
Narrator	And Jesus said to him,
Jesus	**I tell you solemnly, this day, this very night, before the cock crows twice, you will have disowned me three times.**
Narrator	But he repeated still more earnestly,
Peter	If I have to die with you, I will never disown you.
Narrator	And they all said the same.
	They came to a small estate called Gethsemane, and Jesus said to his disciples,
Jesus	**Stay here while I pray.**
Narrator	Then he took Peter and James and John with him. And a sudden fear came over him, and great distress. And he said to them,
Jesus	**My soul is sorrowful to the point of death. Wait here, and keep awake.**
Narrator	And going on a little further he threw himself on the ground and prayed that, if it were possible, this hour might pass him by. He said,
Jesus	**Abba (Father)! Everything is possible for you. Take this cup away from me. But let it be as you, not I, would have it.**
Narrator	He came back and found them sleeping, and he said to Peter,
Jesus	**Simon, are you asleep? Had you not the strength to keep awake one**

9

hour? You should be awake, and praying not to be put to the test. The spirit is willing but the flesh is weak.

Narrator Again he went away and prayed, saying the same words. And once more he came back and found them sleeping, their eyes were so heavy; and they could find no answer for him. He came back a third time and said to them,

Jesus **You can sleep on now and take your rest. It is all over. The hour has come. Now the Son of Man is to be betrayed into the hands of sinners. Get up! Let us go! My betrayer is close at hand already.**

Narrator Even while he was still speaking, Judas, one of the Twelve, came up with a number of men armed with swords and clubs, sent by the chief priests and the scribes and the elders. Now the traitor had arranged a signal with them. He had said,

Judas 'The one I kiss, he is the man. Take him in charge, and see he is well guarded when you lead him away.'

Narrator So when the traitor came, he went straight up to Jesus and said,

Judas Rabbi!

Narrator and kissed him. The others seized him and took him in charge. Then one of the bystanders drew his sword and struck out at the high priest's servant, and cut off his ear.

Then Jesus spoke,

Jesus **Am I a brigand that you had to set out to capture me with swords and clubs? I was among you teaching in the Temple day after day and you never laid hands on me. But this is to fulfil the scriptures.**

Narrator And they all deserted him and ran away. A young man who followed him had nothing on but a linen cloth. They caught hold of him, but he left the cloth in their hands and ran away naked.

They led Jesus off to the high priest; and all the chief priests and the elders and the scribes assembled there. Peter had followed him at a distance, right into the high priest's palace, and was sitting with the attendants warming himself at the fire.

The chief priests and the whole Sanhedrin were looking for evidence against Jesus on which they might pass the death-sentence. But they could not find any. Several, indeed, brought false evidence against him, but their evidence was conflicting. Some stood up and submitted this false evidence against him,

Crowd We heard him say, 'I am going to destroy this Temple made by human hands, and in three days build another, not made by human hands'.

Narrator But even on this point their evidence was conflicting. The high priest then stood up before the whole assembly and put this question to Jesus,

High priest Have you no answer to that? What is this evidence these men are bringing against you?

Narrator But he was silent and made no answer at all. The high priest put a second question to him,

High priest Are you the Christ, the Son of the Blessed One?

Narrator	
Jesus	Jesus said,
	I am, and you will see the Son of Man seated at the right hand of the
Narrator	**Power and coming with the clouds of heaven.**
High priest	The high priest tore his robes, and said,
	What need of witnesses have we now? You heard the blasphemy. What is
Narrator	your finding?
	And they all gave their verdict: he deserved to die.

Some of them started spitting at him and, blindfolding him, began hitting
Crowd him with their fists and shouting,
Narrator Play the prophet!
And the attendants rained blows on him.

While Peter was down below in the courtyard, one of the high
priest's servant-girls came up. She saw Peter warming himself there, stared
Servant-girl at him and said,
Narrator You too were with Jesus, the man from Nazareth.
Peter But he denied it, saying
Narrator I do not know, I do not understand what you are talking about.
And he went out into the forecourt. The servant-girl saw him and again
Servant-girl started telling the bystanders,
Narrator This fellow is one of them.
Crowd But he again denied it. A little later the bystanders themselves said to Peter,
Narrator You are one of them for sure! Why, you are a Galilean.
Peter But he started calling curses on himself and swearing,
Narrator I do not know the man you speak of.
At that moment the cock crew for the second time, and Peter recalled how
Jesus had said to him, 'Before the cock crows twice, you will have disowned
me three times'. And he burst into tears.
► First thing in the morning, the chief priests together with the elders and
scribes, in short the whole Sanhedrin, had their plan ready. They had Jesus
bound and took him away and handed him over to Pilate.

Pilate Pilate questioned him,
Narrator Are you the king of the Jews?
Jesus He answered,
Narrator **It is you who say it.**
And the chief priests brought many accusations against him. Pilate
Pilate questioned him again,
Have you no reply at all? See how many accusations they are bringing against
Narrator you!
But to Pilate's amazement, Jesus made no further reply.

At festival time Pilate used to release a prisoner for them, anyone they
asked for. Now a man called Barabbas was then in prison with the rioters
who had committed murder during the uprising. When the crowd went up
Pilate and began to ask Pilate the customary favour, Pilate answered them,
Narrator Do you want me to release for you the king of the Jews?
For he realised it was out of jealousy that the chief priests had handed Jesus

over. The chief priests, however, had incited the crowd to demand that he should release Barabbas for them instead. Then Pilate spoke again.

Pilate   But in that case, what am I to do with the man you call king of the Jews?

Narrator   They shouted back.

Crowd   Crucify him!

Narrator   Pilate asked them,

Pilate   Why? What harm has he done?

Narrator   But they shouted all the louder,

Crowd   Crucify him!

Narrator   So Pilate, anxious to placate the crowd, released Barabbas for them and, having ordered Jesus to be scourged, handed him over to be crucified.

     The soldiers led him away to the inner part of the palace, that is, the Praetorium, and called the whole cohort together. They dressed him up in purple, twisted some thorns into a crown and put it on him. And they began saluting him,

Crowd   Hail, king of the Jews!

Narrator   They struck his head with a reed and spat on him; and they went down on their knees to do him homage. And when they had finished making fun of him, they took off the purple and dressed him in his own clothes.

     They led him out to crucify him. They enlisted a passer-by, Simon of Cyrene, father of Alexander and Rufus, who was coming in from the country, to carry his cross. They brought Jesus to the place called Golgotha, which means the place of the skull.

     They offered him wine mixed with myrrh, but he refused it. Then they crucified him, and shared out his clothing, casting lots to decide what each should get. It was the third hour when they crucified him. The inscription giving the charge against him read: 'The King of the Jews.' And they crucified two robbers with him, one on his right and one on his left.

     The passers-by jeered at him; they shook their heads and said,

Crowd   Aha! So you would destroy the Temple and rebuild it in three days! Then save yourself: come down from the cross!

Narrator   The chief priests and the scribes mocked him among themselves in the same way. They said,

Crowd   He saved others, he cannot save himself. Let the Christ, the king of Israel, come down from the cross now, for us to see it and believe.

Narrator   Even those who were crucified with him taunted him.

     When the sixth hour came there was darkness over the whole land until the ninth hour. And at the ninth hour Jesus cried out in a loud voice.

Jesus   **Eloi, Eloi, lama sabachthani?**

Narrator   This means 'My God, my God, why have you deserted me?' When some of those who stood by heard this, they said,

Crowd   Listen, he is calling on Elijah.

Narrator   Someone ran and soaked a sponge in vinegar and, putting it on a reed, gave it him to drink, saying,

Bystander   Wait and see if Elijah will come to take him down.

Narrator	But Jesus gave a loud cry and breathed his last.

All kneel and pause a moment.

Narrator	And the veil of the Temple was torn in two from top to bottom. The centurion, who was standing in front of him, had seen how he had died, and he said,
Centurion	In truth this man was a son of God. ◄
Narrator	There were some women watching from a distance. Among them were Mary of Magdala, Mary who was the mother of James the younger, and Joset, and Salome. These used to follow him and look after him when he was in Galilee. And there were many other women there who had come up to Jerusalem with him.

It was now evening, and since it was Preparation Day (that is, the vigil of the sabbath), there came Joseph of Arimathaea, a prominent member of the Council, who himself lived in the hope of seeing the kingdom of God, and he boldly went to Pilate and asked for the body of Jesus. Pilate, astonished that he should have died so soon, summoned the centurion and enquired if he was already dead. Having been assured of this by the centurion, he granted the corpse to Joseph who bought a shroud, took Jesus down from the cross, wrapped him in the shroud and laid him in a tomb which had been hewn out of the rock. He then rolled a stone against the entrance to the tomb. Mary of Magdala and Mary the mother of Joset were watching and took note of where he was laid.

Passion Sunday [Palm Sunday]

YEAR C

*The passion of our Lord Jesus Christ
according to Luke*

22:14 – 23:56

Narrator | When the hour came Jesus took his place at table, and the apostles with him. And he said to them,

Jesus | **I have longed to eat this passover with you before I suffer; because, I tell you, I shall not eat it again until it is fulfilled in the kingdom of God.**

Narrator | Then, taking a cup, he gave thanks and said,

Jesus | **Take this and share it among you, because from now on, I tell you, I shall not drink wine until the kingdom of God comes.**

Narrator | Then he took some bread, and when he had given thanks, broke it and gave it to them, saying,

Jesus | **This is my body which will be given for you; do this as a memorial of me.**

Narrator | He did the same with the cup after supper, and said,

Jesus | **This cup is the new covenant in my blood which will be poured out for you.**

And yet, here with me on the table is the hand of the man who betrays me. The Son of Man does indeed go to his fate even as it has been decreed, but alas for that man by whom he is betrayed!

Narrator | And they began to ask one another which of them it could be who was to do this thing.

A dispute arose also between them about which should be reckoned the greatest, but he said to them,

Jesus | **Among pagans it is the kings who lord it over them, and those who have authority over them are given the title Benefactor. This must not happen with you. No; the greatest among you must behave as if he were the youngest, the leader as if he were the one who serves. For who is the greater: the one at table or the one who serves? The one at table, surely? Yet here I am among you as one who serves!**

You are the men who have stood by me faithfully in my trials; and now I confer a kingdom on you, just as my Father conferred one on me: you will eat and drink at my table in my kingdom, and you will sit on thrones to judge the twelve tribes of Israel.

Simon, Simon! Satan, you must know, has got his wish to sift you all like wheat; but I have prayed for you, Simon, that your faith may not fail, and once you have recovered, you in your turn must strengthen your brothers.

Narrator	He answered,
Peter	Lord, I would be ready to go to prison with you, and to death.
Narrator	Jesus replied,
Jesus	**I tell you, Peter, by the time the cock crows today you will have denied three times that you know me.**
Narrator	He said to them,
Jesus	**When I sent you out without purse or haversack or sandals, were you short of anything?**
Narrator	They answered,
Crowd	No.
Narrator	He said to them,
Jesus	**But now if you have a purse, take it: if you have a haversack, do the same; if you have no sword, sell your cloak and buy one, because I tell you these words of scripture have to be fulfilled in me: He let himself be taken for a criminal. Yes, what scripture says about me is even now reaching its fulfilment.**
Narrator	They said,
Crowd	Lord, there are two swords here now.
Narrator	He said to them,
Jesus	**That is enough!**
Narrator	He then left the upper room to make his way as usual to the Mount of Olives, with the disciples following. When they reached the place he said to them,
Jesus	**Pray not to be put to the test.**
Narrator	Then he withdrew from them, about a stone's throw away, and knelt down and prayed, saying,
Jesus	**Father, if you are willing, take this cup away from me. Nevertheless, let your will be done, not mine.**
Narrator	Then an angel appeared to him coming from heaven to give him strength. In his anguish he prayed even more earnestly, and his sweat fell to the ground like great drops of blood. When he rose from prayer he went to the disciples and found them sleeping for sheer grief. He said to them,
Jesus	**Why are you asleep? Get up and pray not to be put to the test.**
Narrator	He was still speaking when a number of men appeared, and at the head of them the man called Judas, one of the Twelve, who went up to Jesus to kiss him. Jesus said,
Jesus	**Judas, are you betraying the Son of Man with a kiss?**
Narrator	His followers, seeing what was happening, said,
Crowd	Lord, shall we use our swords?
Narrator	And one of them struck out at the high priest's servant, and cut off his right ear. But at this Jesus spoke,
Jesus	**Leave off! That will do!**
Narrator	And touching the man's ear he healed him. Then Jesus spoke to the chief priests and captains of the Temple guard and elders who had come for him. He said,

Jesus	**Am I a brigand that you had to set out with swords and clubs? When I was among you in the Temple day after day you never moved to lay hands on me. But this is your hour; this is the reign of darkness.**
Narrator	They seized him then and led him away, and they took him to the high priest's house. Peter followed at a distance. They had lit a fire in the middle of the courtyard and Peter sat down among them, and as he was sitting there by the blaze a servant-girl saw him, peered at him and said,
Servant-girl	This person was with him too.
Narrator	But he denied it, saying,
Peter	Woman, I do not know him.
Narrator	Shortly afterwards, someone else saw him and said,
Bystander 1	You are another of them.
Narrator	But Peter replied,
Peter	I am not, my friend.
Narrator	About an hour later, another man insisted, saying,
Bystander 2	This fellow was certainly with him. Why, he is a Galilean.
Narrator	Peter said,
Peter	My friend, I do not know what you are talking about.
Narrator	At that instant, while he was still speaking, the cock crew, and the Lord turned and looked straight at Peter, and Peter remembered what the Lord had said to him, 'Before the cock crows today, you will have disowned me three times'. And he went outside and wept bitterly. Meanwhile the men who guarded Jesus were mocking and beating him. They blindfolded him and questioned him, saying,
Crowd	Play the prophet. Who hit you then?
Narrator	And they continued heaping insults on him. When day broke there was a meeting of the elders of the people, attended by the chief priests and scribes. He was brought before their council, and they said to him,
Crowd	If you are the Christ, tell us.
Narrator	He replied,
Jesus	**If I tell you, you will not believe me, and if I question you, you will not answer. But from now on, the Son of Man will be seated at the right hand of the Power of God.**
Narrator	Then they all said,
Crowd	So you are the Son of God then?
Narrator	He answered,
Jesus	**It is you who say I am.**
Narrator	They said,
Crowd	What need of witnesses have we now? We have heard it for ourselves from his own lips.
Narrator	▶ The whole assembly then rose, and they brought him before Pilate. They began their accusation by saying,
Crowd	We found this man inciting our people to revolt, opposing payment of tribute to Caesar, and claiming to be Christ, a king.

Narrator	Pilate put to him this question,
Pilate	Are you the king of the Jews?
Narrator	He replied,
Jesus	**It is you who say it.**
Narrator	Pilate then said to the chief priests and the crowd,
Pilate	I find no case against this man.
Narrator	But they persisted,
Crowd	He is inflaming the people with his teaching all over Judaea; it has come all the way from Galilee, where he started, down to here.
Narrator	When Pilate heard this, he asked if the man were a Galilean; and finding that he came under Herod's jurisdiction he pased him over to Herod who was also in Jerusalem at that time.

Herod was delighted to see Jesus; he had heard about him and had been wanting for a long time to set eyes on him; moreover, he was hoping to see some miracle worked by him. So he questioned him at some length; but without getting any reply. Meanwhile the chief priests and the scribes were there, violently pressing their accusations. Then Herod, together with his guards, treated him with contempt and made fun of him; he put a rich cloak on him and sent him back to Pilate. And though Herod and Pilate had been enemies before, they were reconciled that same day.

Pilate then summoned the chief priests and the leading men and the people. He said,

Pilate	You brought this man before me as a political agitator. Now I have gone into the matter myself in your presence and found no case against him. Nor has Herod either, since he has sent him back to us. As you can see, the man has done nothing that deserves death, so I shall have him flogged and then let him go.
Narrator	But as one man they howled,
Crowd	Away with him! Give us Barabbas!
Narrator	This man had been thrown into prison for causing a riot in the city and for murder.

Pilate was anxious to set Jesus free and addressed them again, but they shouted back.

Crowd	Crucify him! Crucify him!
Narrator	And for the third time he spoke to them,
Pilate	Why? What harm has this man done? I have found no case against him that deserves death, so I shall have him punished and let him go.
Narrator	But they kept on shouting at the top of their voices, demanding that he should be crucified, and their shouts were growing louder.

Pilate then gave his verdict: their demand was to be granted. He released the man they asked for, who had been imprisoned for rioting and murder, and handed Jesus over to them to deal with as they pleased.

As they were leading him away they seized on a man, Simon from Cyrene, who was coming in from the country, and made him shoulder the cross and carry it behind Jesus. Large numbers of people followed him, and of women

Narrator too who mourned and lamented for him. But Jesus turned to them and said,

Jesus **Daughters of Jerusalem, do not weep for me; weep rather for yourselves and for your children. For the days will surely come when people will say, 'Happy are those who are barren, the wombs that have never borne, the breasts that have never suckled!' Then they will begin to say to the mountains, 'Fall on us!'; to the hills, 'Cover us!' For if men use the green wood like this, what will happen when it is dry?**

Narrator Now with him they were also leading out two other criminals to be executed.

When they reached the place called The Skull, they crucified him there and the criminals also, one on the right, the other on the left. Jesus said,

Jesus **Father, forgive them; they do not know what they are doing.**

Narrator Then they cast lots to share out his clothing. The people stayed there watching him. As for the leaders, they jeered at him, saying,

Crowd He saved others; let him save himself if he is the Christ of God, the Chosen One.

Narrator The soldiers mocked him too, and when they approached to offer him vinegar they said,

Crowd If you are the king of the Jews, save yourself.

Narrator Above him there was an inscription: 'This is the King of the Jews.'

One of the criminals hanging there abused him, saying,

Criminal 1 Are you not the Christ? Save yourself and us as well.

Narrator But the other spoke up and rebuked him,

Criminal 2 Have you no fear of God at all? You got the same sentence as he did, but in our case we deserved it: we are paying for what we did. But this man has done nothing wrong. Jesus, remember me when you come into your kingdom.

Narrator He replied

Jesus **Indeed, I promise you, today you will be with me in paradise.**

Narrator It was now about the sixth hour and, with the sun eclipsed, a darkness came over the whole land until the ninth hour. The veil of the Temple was torn right down the middle; and when Jesus had cried out in a loud voice, he said,

Jesus **Father, into your hands I commit my spirit.**

Narrator With these words he breathed his last.

All kneel and pause a moment

Narrator When the centurion saw what had taken place, he gave praise to God and said,

Centurion This was a great and good man.

Narrator And when all the people who had gathered for the spectacle saw what had happened, they went home beating their breasts.

All his friends stood at a distance; so also did the women who had accompanied him from Galilee, and they saw all this happen. ◄

Then a member of the council arrived, an upright and virtuous man named Joseph. He had not consented to what the others had planned and carried out. He came from Arimathaea, a Jewish town, and he lived in the hope of seeing the kingdom of God. This man went to Pilate and asked for the body of Jesus. He then took it down, wrapped it in a shroud and put him in a tomb which was hewn in stone in which no one had yet been laid. It was Preparation Day and the sabbath was imminent.

Meanwhile the women who had come from Galilee with Jesus were following behind. They took note of the tomb and of the position of the body.

Then they returned and prepared spices and ointments. And on the sabbath day they rested, as the law required.

Good Friday

The passion of our Lord Jesus Christ
according to John   18:1 – 19:42

Narrator   Jesus left with his disciples and crossed the Kedron valley. There was a garden there, and he went into it with his disciples. Judas the traitor knew the place well, since Jesus had often met his disciples there, and he brought the cohort to this place together with a detachment of guards sent by the chief priests and the Pharisees, all with lanterns and torches and weapons. Knowing everything that was going to happen to him, Jesus then came forward and said,

Jesus   **Who are you looking for?**

Narrator   They answered,

Crowd   Jesus the Nazarene.

Narrator   He said,

Jesus   **I am he.**

Narrator   Now Judas the traitor was standing among them. When Jesus said, 'I am he', they moved back and fell to the ground. He asked them a second time,

Jesus   **Who are you looking for?**

Narrator   They said,

Crowd   Jesus the Nazarene.

Narrator   Jesus replied,

Jesus   **I have told you that I am he. If I am the one you are looking for, let these others go.**

Narrator   This was to fulfil the words he had spoken: 'Not one of those you gave me have I lost'.

    Simon Peter, who carried a sword, drew it and wounded the high priest's servant, cutting off his right ear. The servant's name was Malchus. Jesus said to Peter,

Jesus   **Put your sword back in its scabbard; am I not to drink the cup that the Father has given me?**

Narrator   The cohort and its captain and the Jewish guards seized Jesus and bound him. They took him first to Annas, because Annas was the father-in-law of Caiaphas, who was high priest that year. It was Caiaphas who had suggested to the Jews, 'It is better for one man to die for the people'.

    Simon Peter, with another disciple, followed Jesus. This disciple, who was known to the high priest, went with Jesus into the high priest's palace, but Peter stayed outside the door. So the other disciple, the one known to the high priest, went out, spoke to the woman who was keeping the door and brought Peter in. The maid on duty at the door said to Peter,

Maid   Aren't you another of that man's disciples?

Narrator   He answered,

Peter	I am not.
Narrator	Now it was cold, and the servants and guards had lit a charcoal fire and were standing there warming themselves; so Peter stood there too, warming himself with the others.
	The high priest questioned Jesus about his disciples and his teaching. Jesus answered,
Jesus	**I have spoken openly for all the world to hear; I always taught in the synagogue and in the Temple where all the Jews meet together; I have said nothing in secret. But why ask me? Ask my hearers what I taught: they know what I said.**
Narrator	At these words, one of the guards standing by gave Jesus a slap in the face, saying,
Guard	Is that the way to answer the high priest?
Narrator	Jesus replied,
Jesus	**If there is something wrong in what I said, point it out; but if there is no offence in it, why do you strike me?**
Narrator	Then Annas sent him, still bound, to Caiaphas, the high priest.
	As Simon Peter stood there warming himself, someone said to him,
Bystander	Aren't you another of his disciples?
Narrator	He denied it saying,
Peter	I am not.
Narrator	One of the high priest's servants, a relation of the man whose ear Peter had cut off, said,
Servant	Didn't I see you in the garden with him?
Narrator	Again Peter denied it; and at once a cock crew.
	They then led Jesus from the house of Caiaphas to the Praetorium. It was now morning. They did not go into the Praetorium themselves or they would be defiled and unable to eat the passover. So Pilate came outside to them and said,
Pilate	What charge do you bring against this man?
Narrator	They replied,
Crowd	If he were not a criminal, we should not be handing him over to you.
Narrator	Pilate said,
Pilate	Take him yourselves, and try him by your own Law.
Narrator	The Jews answered,
Crowd	We are not allowed to put a man to death.
Narrator	This was to fulfil the words Jesus had spoken indicating the way he was going to die.
	So Pilate went back into the Praetorium and called Jesus to him, and asked,
Pilate	Are you the king of the Jews?
Narrator	Jesus replied,
Jesus	**Do you ask this of your own accord, or have others spoken to you about me?**
Narrator	Pilate answered,

21

Pilate: Am I a Jew? It is your own people and the chief priests who have handed you over to me: what have you done?

Narrator: Jesus replied,

Jesus: **Mine is not a kingdom of this world; if my kingdom were of this world, my men would have fought to prevent me being surrendered to the Jews. But my kingdom is not of this kind.**

Narrator: Pilate said,

Pilate: So you are a king then?

Narrator: Jesus answered,

Jesus: **It is you who say it. Yes, I am a king. I was born for this, I came into the world for this; to bear witness to the truth, and all who are on the side of truth listen to my voice.**

Narrator: Pilate said,

Pilate: Truth? What is that?

Narrator: And with that he went out again to the Jews and said,

Pilate: I find no case against him. But according to a custom of yours I should release one prisoner at the Passover; would you like me, then, to release the king of the Jews?

Narrator: At this they shouted:

Crowd: Not this man, but Barabbas.

Narrator: Barabbas was a brigand.
Pilate then had Jesus taken away and scourged; and after this, the soldiers twisted some thorns into a crown and put it on his head, and dressed him in a purple robe. They kept coming up to him and saying,

Crowd: Hail, king of the Jews!
and they slapped him in the face.

Narrator: Pilate came outside again and said to them,

Pilate: Look, I am going to bring him out to you to let you see that I find no case.

Narrator: Jesus then came out wearing the crown of thorns and the purple robe. Pilate said,

Pilate: Here is the man.

Narrator: When they saw him the chief priests and the guards shouted,

Crowd: Crucify him! Crucify him!

Narrator: Pilate said,

Pilate: Take him yourselves and crucify him: I can find no case against him.

Narrator: The Jews replied,

Crowd: We have a Law, and according to the Law he ought to die, because he has claimed to be the son of God.

Narrator: When Pilate heard them say this his fears increased. Re-entering the Praetorium, he said to Jesus,

Pilate: Where do you come from?

Narrator: But Jesus made no answer. Pilate then said to him,

Pilate: Are you refusing to speak to me? Surely you know I have power to release you and I have power to crucify you?

Narrator: Jesus replied

Jesus : **You would have no power over me if it had not been given you from above; that is why the one who handed me over to you has the greater guilt.**

Narrator : From that moment Pilate was anxious to set him free, but the Jews shouted,

Crowd : If you set him free you are no friend of Caesar's; anyone who makes himself king is defying Caesar.

Narrator : Hearing these words, Pilate had Jesus brought out, and seated himself on the chair of judgement at a place called the Pavement, in Hebrew Gabbatha. It was Passover Preparation Day, about the sixth hour. Pilate said to the Jews,

Pilate : Here is your king.

Narrator : They said,

Crowd : Take him away, take him away. Crucify him!

Narrator : Pilate said,

Pilate : Do you want me to crucify your king?

Narrator : The chief priests answered,

Crowd : We have no king except Caesar.

Narrator : So in the end Pilate handed him over to them to be crucified.

They then took charge of Jesus, and carrying his own cross he went out of the city to the place of the skull, or, as it was called in Hebrew, Golgotha, where they crucified him with two others, one on either side with Jesus in the middle. Pilate wrote out a notice and had it fixed to the cross; it ran: 'Jesus the Nazarene, King of the Jews.' This notice was read by many of the Jews, because the place where Jesus was crucified was not far from the city, and the writing was in Hebrew, Latin and Greek. So the Jewish chief priests said to Pilate,

Crowd : You should not write 'King of the Jews', but 'This man said: I am King of the Jews'.

Narrator : Pilate answered,

Pilate : What I have written, I have written.

Narrator : When the soldiers had finished crucifying Jesus they took his clothing and divided it into four shares, one for each soldier. His undergarment was seamless, woven in one piece from neck to hem; so they said to one another,

Crowd : Instead of tearing it, let's throw dice to decide who is to have it.

Narrator : In this way the words of scripture were fulfilled:

They shared out my clothing among them.
They cast lots for my clothes.

This is exactly what the soldiers did.

Near the cross of Jesus stood his mother and his mother's sister, Mary the wife of Clopas, and Mary of Magdala. Seeing his mother and the disciple he loved standing near her, Jesus said to his mother,

Jesus ! **Woman, this is your son.**

Narrator : Then to the disciple he said,

Jesus : **This is your mother.**

23

Narrator And from that moment the disciple made a place for her in his home.

After this, Jesus knew that everything had now been completed, and to fulfil the scripture perfectly he said:

Jesus **I am thirsty.**

Narrator A jar full of vinegar stood there, so putting a sponge soaked in vinegar on a hyssop stick they held it up to his mouth. After Jesus had taken the vinegar he said,

Jesus **It is accomplished;**

Narrator and bowing his head he gave up the spirit.

All kneel and pause a moment

Narrator It was Preparation Day, and to prevent the bodies remaining on the cross during the sabbath – since that sabbath was a day of special solemnity – the Jews asked Pilate to have the legs broken and the bodies taken away. Consequently the soldiers came and broke the legs of the first man who had been crucified with him and then of the other. When they came to Jesus, they found that he was already dead, and so instead of breaking his legs one of the soldiers pierced his side with a lance; and immediately there came out blood and water. This is the evidence of one who saw it – trustworthy evidence, and he knows he speaks the truth – and he gives it so that you may believe as well. Because all this happened to fulfil the words of scripture:

Not one bone of his will be broken,

and again, in another place scripture says:

They will look on the one whom they have pierced.

After this, Joseph of Arimathaea, who was a disciple of Jesus – though a secret one because he was afraid of the Jews – asked Pilate to let him remove the body of Jesus. Pilate gave permission, so they came and took it away. Nicodemus came as well – the same one who had first come to Jesus at night-time – and he brought a mixture of myrrh and aloes, weighing about a hundred pounds. They took the body of Jesus and wrapped it with the spices in linen cloths, following the Jewish burial custom. At the place where he had been crucified there was a garden, and in the garden a new tomb in which no one had yet been buried. Since it was the Jewish Day of Preparation and the tomb was near at hand, they laid Jesus there.